Cleaning a Rainbow

poems

Also by Gary Gildner

Poetry

The Bunker in the Parsley Fields
Clackamas
Blue Like the Heavens: New & Selected Poems
The Runner
Nails
Digging for Indians
First Practice

Limited Editions

The Birthday Party
The Swing
Pavol Hudák, The Poet, Is Talking
Jabón
Letters from Vicksburg
Eight Poems

Fiction

Somewhere Geese are Flying: New & Selected Stories
The Second Bridge
A Week in South Dakota
The Crush

Memoir

My Grandfather's Book: Generations of an American Family
The Warsaw Sparks

Anthology

Out of the World: Poems from the Hawkeye State

Cleaning a Rainbow
poems

Gary Gildner

BkMk Press
University of Missouri-Kansas City

Financial assistance for this project has been provided by
the Missouri Arts Council, a state agency.

Cover art and author photo: Paula Streeter
Book design: Susan L. Schurman
Managing Editor: Ben Furnish
Printing: Walsworth Publishing Co., Marceline, Missouri

BkMk Press wishes to thank Teresa Collins, Emily Iorg, Sandra Meyer,
David E. Rowe, Chelsea Seguin.

Library of Congress Cataloging-in-Publication Data

Gildner, Gary
    Cleaning a rainbow : poems / Gary Gildner.
        p. cm.
    Summary: "This collection of 39 poems features themes of the
relationship between father and daughter--particularly the discoveries that
come to the father of a young girl as the father remembers his own parents
and considers the nature of aging and the value of reminiscence and personal
reflection--includes images of nature and life in the mountains of Idaho."
Provided by publisher.
    ISBN 9781886157637 (pbk.: alk. paper)
I. Title.
    PS3557 .I343 C57 2007
    811' / .54--dc22
                                        2007029628

This book is set in Adobe Jenson Pro, Sand, and Optima type.

Acknowledgements

Certain poems in this book first appeared in the following publications:

Artful Dodge: "The 1902 Dime," "The Mixer," "A Wooden Sword," "The Mail" (as "Getting the Mail"), "Translating My Polish Mother," "Around the Corral" and "Christina."

Brilliant Corners: "The Gig."

The Georgia Review: "In Development No. 3," "Happiness Jazz," "Joseph Shows Up for the Christmas Story Three Days After His Hernia Repair" and "The Summer Afternoon."

Horse People (Artisan Books): "After Straddling the Granary Roof."

The Kenyon Review: "A New Song" and "In Pioneer Park (*later*)."

Maxis Review: "A Little Portrait."

New Letters: "Ella," "The Hand," "Visitation Night, Dinner for Two" and "Writer to Writer."

Orion: "Cleaning a Rainbow."

The Paris Review: "Enter the North Dakota Librarian"

Petroglyph: "Rock Tea."

Poetry Northwest: "Robespierre," "My Wife and Daughter Are Rolling Snow as I Write by the Window," "The Birthday Party," "Measuring" and "Thistles."

Portland: "Three."

The Prose Poem: An International Journal: "Days of 1952."

Shenandoah: "Weak Strong."

The Southern Review: "'Interior with a Maroon Sofa.'"

Weber Studies: "The Fish Dog," "Where the Dog is Buried" and "The Ingt."

Witness: "All This."

Harry N. Abrams, Inc., first published "A Word" in the anthology *Heart to Heart* (2001), ed. by Jan Greenberg.

Special thanks to Rick and Rosemary Ardinger of Limberlost Press who printed eleven of these poems in a letterpress limited edition, *The Birthday Party*, in the spring of 2000.

"To Margaret" first appeared in the Limberlost Postcard Series.

Cleaning
ᵃ Rainbow
p o e m s

I

II

III

"It takes me that long to get everything in."

—John Coltrane's response to Miles Davis
about why he took such long solos.

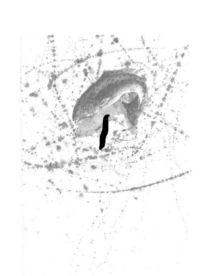

1

ALL THIS

When we go out walking,
my daughter and I,
just to go walking,
and she finds a stone
she never saw before,
a flat yellow muddy stone
with brown veins snaking through,
and holds it close to her chest
as she was held fresh from the womb,
and says she must take it home
for my birthday,
to put a candle on it and blow
until everyone is happy,
and on the way sets it carefully down
among the excited bees around her feet,
because we've discovered some wild
strawberries ready to pick
and pick them, feeling those
tiny surprising bursts in our mouths
we never expected,
and can't describe except by flapping our elbows,
and then continue on up the mountain
until the stone is settled
beside my place at the table—
I don't much care if
all this began
as a smooth, hot soup
billions of years ago,
or got cleverly whipped up
by One with a fabulous sense of humor.
I just don't want it to stop very soon.

THE GIG

They invited me in, then
asked what I played.
I said horn. They
handed me one with a long cord
hanging down. They said
sample it, man. I
put the small round end
to my mouth and blew—
it was okay. Unusual
but okay. Then the guy
on sax tapped out one, two,
one, two, three and we started.
He was good, he grew large
wings, wings and a deep concern.
Everyone stopped, including me.
The question seemed to be:
where were we?
I felt bad. My timing
was slow, the sound
I pushed out full of
wet air, farty.
And that cord kept
getting underfoot.
But I wasn't going to
make excuses. My horn
was a damn lamp
with a yellow shade.
My lips were sore.
So what? This was the gig.
Let's go, I said. Let's play.

ROBESPIERRE

Here's to the rooster Robespierre
who is getting ready,
who is beside himself
admiring and full
and not to be denied,
who, refused first prize
at the Idaho County Fair
for a single feather stuck out wayward
in his rich, rust-colored tail,
is throwing back his head now, is letting go
loud and pure enough to raise all manner
of lovers, not only farmers constantly moved by morning
but angels too, flushed, loosed from conjugal eiderdown wrap
and haystack, from sweat-slickened horse tack and rodeo straw
tossed in the box of a pickup—crowing, crowing across
the Camas prairie and beyond is grand Robespierre,
to the Sawtooths, the Seven Devils, Hell's Canyon, and the Gospels
catching moose bowing in their first delicious browse,
catching young boys shaken and rolled
from silky, shimmering dreams into their backbones,
catching the wild turkey blinking above his wattles, catching even
the politician cowering, confused by such clear, inspired song—
husky, sky-throated Robespierre the unbeatable, complete bird
holding his bent, independent feather up high,
here's to you and the quickened day,
the day uncommon, touched, gloriously breaking.

THREE

She knocks on my door, says,
"Papa, I have a question—
what about when I was a baby?"

I let her in. She's wearing an orange
bathing suit over a plum-blue
bathing suit, her hands and cheeks are

smeared green with watercolor, on her
head a billed cap tilts back
like my dad's carpenter's cap

tilted back at the end of a hard day,
and around her neck a string of paper
pine trees held together

by Band-Aids dangles down—
"I'm trying to remember and I have to
tell you," she says, "it's never easy."

THE 1902 DIME

My mother, always dramatic,
    sends me a note—
        "Here you go, brother,

one thin dime
    I can spare—good luck."
        It's so worn down

Miss Liberty's hard
    to make out. Is that a bun
        of hair she wears? Or a cap

like the gauzy affair
    my grandmother tied on
        to keep off dust? Do

the ribbons trailing away
    from her neck wrap
        both or neither?

Her chin starts and gives up,
    her lips are a nick
        and unkissable,

her nose is nearly rubbed
    flat, her eye a fly-
        speck of dark at the bridge,

and the raised letters "UNITED
    STATES
        OF AMERICA"

almost circling her head
    are almost not there.
        However, "1902"

at the bottom stands up
    so clear
        I can even see green,

grainy, smoky Detroit
    in the spring of that year.
        Stefan Szostak, immigrant

Pole, blacksmith, lays down
    his tongs, takes the hand of
        Aniela. Clove and laurel

sweeten their way. "Always
    and everywhere,"
        he sings, from Mickiewicz,

"I remain by your side." Close by
    on West Forest Avenue
        Lindbergh—Lucky Lindy—

is a brand new baby, and farther away
    the famous Animal
        Crackers box—

designed to look like a car
    in Barnum's circus train—
        is likewise new.

What a moving year, 1902!
    In the wedding photo
        everyone holds

very still, as if stopped dead
    on a dime in wonder.
        Hail Columbia! My mother,

their seventh child, comes along
    shaking her sunny hair,
        unable to stop

dancing, dreaming of being
    a star, shimmering
        like a million, like platinum

blonde Jean Harlow and all
    those other swell-
        looking well-heeled dames.

She dances still, at eighty-two,
    the polka, the Lindy—even
        the fuddy fox-trot. Call her

anything you like,
    she says, so long
        as it's *lucky*—a word

I grew up hearing
    clicking its tiny
        nails

around the house
    like a mouse
        we needed to trap.

The dime I hold
    for years went to work
        in my carpenter father's

lunch pail, "tucked away,"
    she writes, "under that burning
        oh my god

sandwich
    he loved so much."
        I remember

his wink
    at taking the first slow
        crackling bite—

a big slice of onion
        and mashed
                horseradish root

captured by thick, dark
        old-country bread
                made with potatoes

by her, by way of Aniela,
        while swaying to something smooth
                on the radio—and afterwards

the little snooze
        under his cap, a fresh nailbag
                his pillow.

But the dime she tucked
        in the pail—
                for luck, for the day

their ship came in, when
        she could just imagine him
                waltzing home

smoking a fancy
        ten-cent cigar—
                I do not remember.

DAYS OF 1952

His status in our parish was that of a visitor who didn't have anywhere to go, we heard, and the pastor took him in. A refugee. But he was always smiling. Always. We preferred him for Confession to even young Father Albert, the regular assistant (who drove a very clean pre-war Studebaker), because we thought he didn't really understand us and therefore never gave more than five Hail Marys or five Our Fathers as a penance. He was German and bald and stooped over, and his crooked fingers looked like roots. For recreation, he grew tomatoes behind the rectory garage. He never wore street clothes, just the black soutane. Never drove a car or had little jokes for the altar boys before Mass, or ever really talked with us. It was the English, we said. Yet he seemed delighted with everything, even with saying, week after week, the five o'clock Sunday morning Mass that mainly old women and the drinkers attended. He always had the longest line waiting for him at Saturday Confessions and got through it fast. We laughed about that. We went to him with our worst sins. We figured everybody did.

THE MIXER

Angus the mixer stood above us
stirring cream and milk and powdered yolk
until the big vat's sweetened soup
thickened on his fingertip
just the way he liked it—
then he licked it, slow, the furrow
in his brow a thinker's ditch.
This was how he talked.
"Angus is a careful man who weighs
and ponders every move he makes.
Pay attention, boys, ice cream's
only part of it." He told us several times
each night how this or that out there beyond
our second shift had profit in it,
or was worthless, why,
and what we ought to do
was watch him, listen when he spoke
and not forget. "Angus," he would say
atop his perch—and poke the licked
digit at us—"Angus the mixer
is your captain, gents. Take notes."
We were high school kids
making summer money—
we thought the guy was funny.
Have I told this story? How forty
years ago a door left open
let a light-crazed, whirling mob
of June bugs dive inside and join
the fresh-made creamy mix?
All six of us, including Angus,
simply watched. It happened fast—
the night's batch ruined. I thought
of that again hearing something
on the news about a giant outfit
selling rat-contaminated food—and then

of how our captain saved the day
by dumping sacks of nuts and chocolate
syrup in the vat and barking, "Right,
we're boxing Double Crunch Delight tonight!"
I remember how we howled approval,
how the job went by so fast
we would've had the time, afterwards, to call
our girlfriends, go out, park, get lost
among the stars, the smells
of summer on our skins' sweet rubbings,
and become some kind of kings.
Instead, the night already rich enough,
I guess, the five of us
went somewhere else, some field, and drank
the Jumbos Angus bought, and laughed
at how our little world worked.
And said that one day, God
damn it, we were leaving Flint—
sailing clear, no graduating into smelly
shop rat life for us, no punching in,
punching out, and maybe wondering,
underneath, who or what in hell
we really were. I remember how
the moon slid down, close and full,
and how we raced around for stones to hit it
when the beer was gone.

THISTLES

In the humid heat
following a week's rain,
I pulled thistles off
a slope, the slim
Canadian bearing that
purple blossom
horses love to eat,
working their lips just so
like the toothless old.
I wanted them up
from the root
before they ripened
into seed. Released
from the house,
from writing words
I had no feelings for,
sticky with sweat,
I was happy.
I remembered lathered
horses I had known,
how like fresh crushed
oats they always smelled,
how the hard block of salt
I chipped a sliver off
from the cup their tongues licked out
tasted hot,
how I broke
my leg sliding over
mud into third, the sharp
finger-snapping
sound it made—
and then the hiss
of a water pipe
returned, a furnace
beside us, Delphine Bononi's

woolly rabbit-fur sweater
pressing my heartbeat.
Where was I?
As if caught
in the softest of dream
falls, I was stopped, wrapped,
and brought back
to start over.
Slowly. Up here. Now.
No perfect tumble
into sleep after fierce
play, no race to raise
my arm and shout
from the highest, most
willowy limb, no dive
daring my hilarious lungs
to hold out, hold out
against the river, not one
of the world's roaring gifts
I knew
compared to this, my first
real kiss. It
changed the meaning
of my mouth,
the way I took
small or great
breaths forever,
and if only for an instant
it flared in the rippling mountain
heat surrounding me, alive
as anything given up
wholly to a pure
shimmer
already slipping
away,
intact as nothing
I could hold, a current
leaving and leaving behind
in the bright bone

oven of my aging skull
one cool, finny,
adolescent shiver.
Sometime later
I had to laugh,
remembering the fiery
sulfurous stink
and sad shriveled-up look
of my leg
after the cast
came off.
And later still,
gripping the clay
slope on my knees,
I returned to the chore
I had come there for,
now and then stopping
to watch a bee
riding a blossom,
a hawk soaring
under the sun.

THE MAIL

Mid-March and the mountain's dirt trail
I walk up, holding the pups' leads, is soupy—
flecks of isinglass glint at my feet, the sun cuts
among slim tamarack, limbs snow-bowed for days
slowly swing back—a jay jumps, rails
on a stump and is gone. Under my shirt
a letter from my mother says, "Look—for once
you are not moving." It's true, in black and white
the old Brownie snap shows Eddie the Z. and me
standing still.

          I am tempted to stop
and look at us again, at our mock-drunk grins and tipped
sailor hats and the grapevines over our shoulders
lush as cabbages, at the pear tree loaded with fruit—
and beyond all that the figure of a man
way in the gray background who must be my father
just home from work. He must be wearing
overalls, a pencil pushed under his carpenter's cap—
watching this moment more than forty years ago,
caught there at the far corner where house, vines and tree
and he himself all seem to be falling into each other—
caught there by my mother, who is trying to catch
something closer.

          But I don't
take out her gift again, because suddenly I see
a flock of turkeys—thirty—I count them—thirty
wild turkeys mincing over Bailey's muddy pasture.
At first they look like turtles somehow in high heels—
then, fluffed up, sharp as the hat Admiral Nelson
turned just so during his heydays. They seem
in no great hurry, though here and there one makes
a fussy little spurt as if hissed at to get in formation.
But the quickest, jerkiest motions come from

the toms, shaking their wattles—
bags of red flesh so freshly bright
they might have been dipped in paint
only seconds before I showed up.
I have never seen such a bunch, and crouch
down level with my pups' pricked ears,
hoping to see more: a battle, a dance—
at the moment I can't remember what they do
to determine the top cock.

                    Now,
starting to complain about something—
me? my dogs?—they send up gargled hoots, screams
of halfhearted outrage, and move away, closer and closer
to the safe cover of a cedar copse bordering Bailey's pasture.
I watch them go, old dowagers on nice pensions, consorts
heading for port flapping their jibs, know-it-all
rednecks cheek by jowl with self-made millionaires
who know it all too, philosophers, wags, coupon-clippers—
"Is this the life?" I ask my dogs, feeling giddy,
feeling the tension in their flanks to take off, pursue,
and run until the running comes down to a dish
of fresh water, a slow comforting curl...

Two of us in that yard I carry
are gone, though if I reach under my shirt,
which I can at any moment,
we will all be there, still,
or still enough, falling together
near the end of summer, among summer's produce,
faithfully practicing how to come out.

MEASURING

Margaret finds me in my father's garden
out behind the house—a field, now,
of weeds and grasses that are beautiful to her.
She is five and takes her time choosing
this one, this one, making up their names—
Charlotte, Henry Fox, Elizabeth. Oh, and *this* one
is the prize.

                The prize? Yes, the flower
we don't really have a name for.
I think to say she's picked a stalk of timothy
but I stop myself. Nor do I say that thirty
years ago my father, turning up the dirt, right here,
fell, and did not stand again.

                    I say he built
that house, an apple tree he planted brushed
the windows where I slept. I say he kept
a pencil underneath his cap, or halfway underneath,
to measure with.

             Measure what? Oh, lots of things,
even kids. For example, like I measure you.
All this pleases her. She reminds me how,
for example, she herself can almost reach
the apple tree outside *her* room at home.
And how, for example, she just needs to
get away sometimes—and grow.

                She takes my hand.
We're a hair rich and half poor—that's how
lucky we are! She turns, alive
with happiness, and whirling
lets me go.

CLEANING A RAINBOW

I open it with my long blade under the bright flow
of well water and there lie the finny wings
a moth is beginning to fold,
and then I see the river again, and where I stood
in sun- and rain-slant, that arc of color, the trout
coming down, pulling everything with it, the cold mountain
stream, the boulders blue and yellow and red, pines wind-pushed
among them and scrubbed to a silvery finish, current-salved, their limbs
lashed by tendrils of pale canary grass, all inside it and coming down,
the veined pebbles inside it and coming down, rolling, even the pearly
stone a raw-throated raven kicked loose, the lovesick bray
a wandering mule gave out causing a moose at first-
light browse to look up, the moony call
an owl still can't stop giving softly inside it, the slow-waking
kayaker's deep satisfying sleep washed from her eyes vividly inside it,
all inside it and coming down, finding their places, the feathered layers
of flesh making room, the pursy fir and lean young alders
in league with the willows, all bending, their refusals to snap
quietly folded inside it, their needles and leaves and aspirations, too
subtle to separate, completely inside it, tracks large and showy
and barely there become petite, hair-thin bones, become murmuring
rib-chimes, choirs, echoes from the lightest touch inside it and coming
down the river, embraced by the scent of cherry and musk, by the shy
fairy slipper, by bear's breath and the must oozing
from a single wild grape, by incense cedar, myrtle
and skittish skunk, all rank and sweet together, all
brushings and sighs coming down, through slick spidery worm-scrawl
falling, flicker-knock, locked horn and cocky treble-cry falling, famous
stalkings and leaps lost in the furling eddies, the heart sucked
under, fibril and seed and viscid yolk sucked under, necks
nuzzled, licked, whirling around astonished, dogtooth violet and thorny
rosebush torn from their root mesh, garnishing all, and everyone rushing
down, down to this small washing, this curl of final composure
I hold in the bowl of my hands kneeling to receive it.

HAPPINESS JAZZ

Okay, that number comes up
with or without much help.
Mothers, brothers, friends, all
kinds of people—kind, cruel,
little kids when you least
expect it—ask for it. First
thing the morning after hard
self-abuse, even you've had
the urge to wish for a bite.
Even old Franklin, the crafty kite
guy, said Hey, wait a minute,
when T.J. wrote *life, liberty,*
and the protection of property.
Said we want the pursuit
of something that juices.
Like sex, like food, like Jesus
and rime, time hasn't put
much of a stop, much of a boot
to its chops. Teeth, baby, it's got
molars, precious metals, fangs,
a grip that won't quit, lungs,
lug nuts, sunsets, dawns dappled
and crippled, shims missing, trouble
in mind, howls, oh no's, new shoes
that slide & glide, sass, the blues
to bring a person around exactly
when he or she's down inexactly.
Come on, B-flat, lift that head so
heavy, that heart so full,
break through and spill
over, way over, honey,
let go and grab hold
as if you had *all* the money.

MY WIFE AND DAUGHTER ARE ROLLING SNOW
AS I WRITE BY THE WINDOW

from time to time
changing the seasons, the tune

I put down pulling carrots last autumn
I put down pulling back the summer river, wading in

giving the river its length of green evening light
giving the late carrots their delicate white hairs

I remember laying my line
over the same pebbled eddy, over and over

I remember two parrots
perched on fingers far away

Day-O, day-O, Amos...
Nipper, Nipper, Nipper...

the rare Calypso orchid
is also called Fairy Slipper

we found one last spring
blooming near Margaret's swing, only feet

from where the deer
often lie in the night

they are rolling a head now
exposing another path of grass

laughing, lifting it up
hoist her / oyster

Margaret yells, "Carrots! We need carrots!"
the cat Yah teh appears, sits down to observe

Lizzie reaches for her, a leg thrown back, ballet-like, nice
Margaret simply bends, gathering

together they raise the pliant cat
closer to their moony round smiling man

like that
these things happen

and will never happen again

WRITER TO WRITER

Bringing me a sheet of paper
and a pencil, my daughter
wants to see how "her" looks,
exactly. I make it.
"Now," she says, "do *here*."
I place it under the other and call
attention to the subtle rhyme.
"Do *ear*." I say, "Very nice."
She pauses a moment to think, holding
a finger over her lips. "*Kiss*."
I write it down, saying, "I see
you're favoring the senses."
"Don't confuse me." "Okay."
"Now *caring?*" "Yes, indeed," I say,
keeping the question mark
I heard to myself. "Ah,"
she says quietly, soberly,
"I've got it. *Heart*."
When I finish crossing the *t*
she takes the paper and checks
everything out, humming a little
underscore for each word. A hum,
I wonder, with a touch
of uncertainty? I want to ask
if she is happy with the result.
I want to say, If you're not,
it's perfectly normal. Life is difficult
to put into words. You can even
miss it completely and years
will go by, *good* years
you've never given a chance
because you're brooding, brooding—
and one day, one beautiful ordinary day
like all the others, you discover how hard
you've been on yourself. Darling girl,

please don't—don't what? Don't live
like that? So turned inward, so—?
"Dad," she says, looking at me, "you've
done a good job with this." Looking
both hard and soft,
and it must be, I think, it must be.

A WORD

Give me I said to those round
young faces a round word
and they looked at me
fully puzzled until finally
several cried What do you mean?

I mean I said round round
you know about round
and Oh yes they said but
give us examples!

Okay I said let's have a
square word
square maybe
will lead us to round.

And they groaned
they groaned and they frowned
every one except one
little voice way in the back said
Toast.

THE INGT

Sometimes I'll take a word out of the blue
to see how many words are inside it,
like I'm doing with *Washington*,
where I happen to find myself now.
Wash and *ash* and *shin*, *as* and *in*, man
it's loaded, *on* and *to* and *ton*, a friendly *hi*
in the middle, though *was*, right off the bat,
is waving, one might imagine, goodbye. And then
there's the shy, small, dun-colored *ingt*
I almost missed, that feeds on the tough and stringy
but honey-sweet *hin* flower, which followers of this rare
creature agree is the key to its survival—a bird in fact
that's often mistaken, by amateurs, for an aberrant newt
or frog. It flies, yes, unfurling surprising pastel
wings, finer than silk, but only once, when afraid.
Thus it leaps up, flying, higher and higher, until
its tiny heart, barely bigger than a blackberry seed, bursts,
and down it swirls, slowly, light from the sun or the moon
or the stars caught in those delicate petals
and softly thrown in every direction. Devotees
of the ingt are few, a handful, their personalities marked
by restraint, a certain scarlet swatch in the cheek
appearing when hearing the little bird's plaintive *fee fee*
at mating time (after which the male crowns himself with mud)—
backing away from further intercourse, withdrawing
into the bush, where we might glimpse them quietly crouching
over the chewy hin, their principal nourishment.
Seeing the brilliant death once, they say, is enough.

THE BIRTHDAY PARTY

A full day's walk
from my chopping block
The Gospels lie
softened by snow—
a pearly, generous sky
promising more.
Supple as lovers
taking their time,
they fold into each other
the rough mounds
buffed and powdered,
mouths hidden, lips
making a sound
I think must be *oh*...
"Listen," I say, and
sitting beside me
on the scored block,
gazing that way,
Lizzie listens. It's so
quiet, so large beyond us
I nearly miss her
whisper brushing my ear.
"Someone should scatter
our ashes up there..."
She's come fresh
from her bath, through
apple and plum leaves
blowzy, spiraling
easily down.
In the sandbox
at the garden's edge
our daughter is shaping
cinnamon cakes for
Cheyenne and Seth,
her dear old friends

Ralph the elf brings around
now and again.
"We're so happy
to join you—so thrilled—
Father is sixty, you see—
I'm making him tea..."
Moving in and out
of various voices,
spreading a cloth, gracious,
offering cups, saucers,
a selection of leaves
to pat their lips. Barely
glancing up when
two ravens take off
from a knobcone pine
as if set on fire,
throats racking
We're here! We're here!
The cat Yah teh appears
as always, without fanfare,
like her name—"hello"
in Navajo—and blinks
those bountiful eyes
at Lizzie, at me, at the
pearly sky passing by,
the ravens circling, rasping
in a world curling
around so peacefully.
Finally they quit.
"Look," Lizzie says,
"Yah teh's our guide.
What an angel."
Neither one rushing—
having fun. Walking
with the almost frozen
motions of blush-filled
children pretending to be
very, very sly.
Quietly I stand.

I leave the ax, my chore,
the sweet scent of fir
sap in the air.
I must follow them
and the afternoon's fine
drift, though I want to
move even slower
through the garden—
like sand, like coarse
gravel caught in a long
pearly embrace—rolling up,
settling down among
Cheyenne and Seth
and the gifted Ralph,
and a cat with new-green
glorious eyes who simply
arrived one snowy day,
a skinny little sack
of bones, to adopt us,
that we might say,
dreamily now,
hello, hello,
and again hello.

THE FISH DOG

The children went down to the river and took along Oliver, their fish dog, who possessed an extraordinary nose and equally surprising eyes and ears for anything cold-blooded with fins. He could hold a point like a saint, not moving a muscle until someone threw in a line and got a bite. As soon as the fish was hooked, Oliver began to sing. When he sang an Irish pub song, for example, everybody knew the fish would be fabulous; when he sang a lullaby they knew it would be too small and they'd have to toss it back. Tunes with a jazzy treatment, like "On the Sunny Side of the Street," always meant the fish would be just right and made them feel especially lucky all over. Sometimes he'd sing a deeply emotional song of love or of tragedy from one of the great operas. These were unusual passages—subtle yet demanding—when the children were starting to leave childhood. At such crucial moments Oliver sang his heart out, and hearing him it was difficult to remember the fish; indeed, landing the fish seemed irrelevant, even foolish. No one knew when the crisis would come. That's why Oliver's gift was kept a secret by the children, who often pretended he didn't exist.

FROG ON THE MOUNTAIN

Working late one night in his satchel
   of syllables, thimbles and thread, said—
      as often as he did—"Seems I ought to
deliver a brand new word."

Hopped down through dewy
   dogtooth violets and wild
      plums early next morning
to bring us the word.

Wearing a bluebell leaf for a hat!
   Did he surprise old Mr. Goat
      dribbling lady's slippers off
his whiskers? I'd say so!

Plus, a whole hillside of lilies,
   making an unsticking, almost gooey smack,
      stuck out their faces
because lilies are like that.

Keep hopping, little frog,
   hold on to your hat and your brand new
      word, and don't forget O please don't
let us *lose* you.

Well, he hopped past this mob of bees, see?
   But they didn't see him, because
      they were terribly busy going round
and round trying to choose.

Also, they wanted to tell on tell on tell on
   Momma Bear up to her
      hoggy chops in the berries already.
(Did they tell? Yes, but only on each other.)

Little frog soon came to this tremendously long
    fallen tree—or not *quite*
        fallen, for its bushy limbs
    were kind of catching it.

Frog paused a moment: that's a
    rather nice fall, he thought—
        and if I were a tree coming down
    that's how I'd like to fall. *Soft.*

Closing his eyes, he gave the tree a sniff
    up near the top, where a very small hole
        let his nose poke though.
    He said, "Why, inside it's beautiful!

Like grass and clover closer to the sky. Like
    drifting around. Like tap-tap, hello-hello
        on a rainy night when I feel a tad
    damp and almost alone."

And the thing was, he could spell
    this beautiful smell
        right there, with or without
    paper and pencil.

He spelled it all the way around himself,
    like you and I spell *leaf*
        and *bluebell* and *hat* and *Margaret*
    and *four and a half.*

Then the frog who could spell
    hopped off, careful not to spill
        even one syllable of his brand new word
    which you know to be beautiful.

Like yes. Like guess who? Like the sun now
    fully up, dear Margaret, the sun
        that will break your heart
    in time, as it breaks mine,

Lingering this brief while
  to show you the way,
    wanting stories, frogs, all
things true and beautiful

Not to fade, O my brightness.

TO MARGARET
(who said to me when she was five)

"I'd rather have a turtle
than a horse."

"Why?"

"Well, for lots of reasons.
For one, the sky.
A turtle would never knock you off its back
and make you lie there wondering
how far everything was."

AFTER STRADDLING THE GRANARY ROOF

I sat on Nelly's broad brown powerful back,
holding her bristly mane, smelling that
warm-woodsy-wet-oats skin, and yes,
there *was* a better perch from which to view eternity—
or at least the thing that it seems
will go on forever—
even though we only went slowly round and round
and eventually stopped.

ROCK TEA

At a hot springs in the Sawtooth Mountains
   8,000 feet above the level sea,
my two-year-old daughter enters the steamy shallows, and sings
   I'm naked! I'm naked! And clings to herself
as if the pink body under her slender arms might slip away.
   I do not want her to slip away, not ever,
but I know one day she will. I know
   one day she will put on her snow boots
and take up the trail in earnest—and I will call out
   I am happy for her, very happy, but sad too,
and hope I will see her again. From the pool's moony wash
   she brings me her cupped hands. Rock tea, Papa, you like some?
I cup her hands in my own, and drink. It is delicious, I say,
   more delicious than air itself, than life, may I have another?
And perhaps you will have one too? Perhaps, thank you.
   In this way, gently over rock tea,
we celebrate how far we have traveled together.

"INTERIOR WITH MAROON SOFA"

—oil painting by Galen Hansen

In a museum in Great Falls, Montana,
I looked at this picture and it wasn't the sofa
I fixed on at first but the giant green grasshopper
on the sofa's back, perched up there at least twice
the sofa's size.
                    Then I noticed a man, small,
sitting below, in jeans, boots, buckskin-type shirt
and a big sombrero. He wasn't even
up to the sofa's top. He was looking our way,
this little hombre, with a face so dark it was hard
to read. Was he relaxed as his crossed legs
suggested? Or afraid? waiting? tense?

Or wondering, as I was now, about life's cartoonish
turns, its odd, sometimes unbelievable relationships.
Maybe the grasshopper was an invited guest, a boon
companion, and they were simply enjoying a moment
at home, as anyone and his guest/friend/pet might,
and to heck with the rest of the world.
Or maybe the thing was a huge surprise
and he didn't know, for sure, what was going on
except that he was smaller than he thought.
I didn't know, at the time, that my wife, also looking
at the picture, was seeing another man. At her church,
and afterwards for lunch. Then things just grew. I knew
only what I saw—a giant green grasshopper
perched above a man, both occupying a stately maroon sofa
in a boxlike yellow room.
                    Where a neat little fire
of sticks burned camplike on the floor,
its smoke flowing smoothly out the room's only window.

IN DEVELOPMENT NO. 3

After the revolution I was standing on a balcony with my hosts when a man from above us came flying down. His shadow passed over several balconies across the way like a black ribbon, a streamer, and met him in the street. People walking to and fro gave the body plenty of room, as if it might suddenly spring upon them. Out of the silence, a siren—sounding more like someone practicing a calliope, trying, over and over, to complete a happy line. This stopped when a van arrived. White-coated attendants removed the body. Then women appeared on the balconies around us pinning up diapers and shirts, brushing their hair; men came out to smoke, resting their arms casually along the railings. One at the highest level—he wore an undershirt, a fedora— picked up a small child and they leaned over the railing together, gazing down at older children playing in the street. No voices were raised anywhere. The children, especially, seemed so quiet they might have been challenged to see who could hold his tongue the longest. I didn't know what to say myself. Finally—stupidly—I asked my hosts the name of this street. One shrugged. Another said it was the name of a distant mountain, or an herb on the mountain, she couldn't remember which. All of them agreed it was only a name, like all the other names assigned without thought to such places, and meant nothing.

ELLA

Hiking through the timber sometimes I still
see Ella, a flash of black and tan flank I know
can't be her, yet I pause, always, and listen,
my gaze in that fleeting direction. I stop,
at least I think I do, out of brief confusion:
it wasn't Henry—Henry remained at my side—
but what other creature looked like her? Ran hard
like her, low and lean? A coyote? wolf? mountain lion?
The truth is no animal, nothing flashed by or quick
Henry would have said so. And on we go, if in fact
we ever stop. Yes, I tell myself, I'm getting older.
I spend a lot of time alone. That I once kept a dog
like Ella, whose spirit I loved, who drove me crazy too
because she refused to mind, means what, exactly,
as we make our way? She was the last
of the litter, a runt whom nobody, the owner said,
looked at twice. After selecting Henry, I took her
and she took me. If she learned anything she learned it
only for the treat and promptly forgot—or didn't care.
Those beautiful pearly black eyes—from the Rottweiler father—
she knew how to use on me, after dragging home
another bloody rag of fur. She ran deer, for a while
even enticed Henry along (though he really wanted to mind—
you could see it later in his smoky remorseful eyes).
I tried everything—the leash, more affection, the rolled-up
newspaper, books; nothing took; nothing won her
attention for long except Henry, who got
the Australian shepherd mother's softest parts,
which Ella loved to touch: crawling into a spoon-curl
with the accommodating brother on his bale
of straw in the sun, rarely using her own. At will
she jumped the kennel and came home smelling foul
about the face, poor Henry pacing, pacing
until they lay wrapped in their common house,
peaceful as lovers. The times she got sick
I nursed her back, at first saying I was sorry
to see her like this, later on calling her a bitch.

"*Now* will you learn?" She never did. Hanging around
the yard, as Henry did, was not her idea of being
a dog, and the rope now holding her there made us all mournful.
But that was the story, I told her. "You've got something
nothing seems to fix." I found no joy, felt
no victory in the long hours she lay looking old
in the grass, how she'd nibble a little, notice
a nuthatch work its fussy way down a larch
and then lose interest. She refused
to get in my truck to go see the vet, and bit
my hand when I tried to pick her up.
"She's into self-pity," he laughed on the phone,
"just needs a little time to go by is all."
Weeks went by. Looking at each other we were not
betrayed or estranged or even fellow prisoners,
it was worse, I thought, this thing for which no word
seemed good or bad enough. One evening I was chopping wood.
Perhaps behind those bright, despairing eyes she understood
the way before I did—no doubt I'm rationalizing now—
but she came and stood as far as the rope would reach,
stood very still and so close to me, gazing down
at nothing much—chips of bark, dying dandelions—all
I had to do was turn the ax to its blunt edge,
and without hate or love or anything
nearly so clear, blacken my mind a moment.

A WOODEN SWORD

Some days I take my *bokken,*
cut from a cherry tree,
and slash at the mountain air.
I am Okamoto, the old Master,
and no one messes with me.
But though my face
says one thing, the truth is
I know so little about this
slow hacking away, this sweet dance.
Only that my sword curves upward
and is light, my limbs still work.
Look how those apples fall,
those clouds give way.
Observe how I fight my worst enemies,
my best friends.
How I pray.

THE HAND

When the Skilsaw suddenly bit through the board dropping
straight down I thrust my free hand that reflex I had
as a wiry boy to gather in anything skipping caroming close
soft hands my coaches all said you've got soft hands kid
it's hard now seeing my eager soft hand reaching under
a live blade but what's unclear vague when it's all
very much there?
                Everything was there sharp
the slant of sun on the limp angle those four fingers
took from the perfect crease across my palm how bright
my lifeline that sting the dumb dangle pointing
at the floor littered with sawdust red BBs sun-
freckling around my thumb in a patty of raw flesh
it was important I lay the saw I still held lay it slowly
down keeping the blade away and then see to this new
arrangement half my hand had taken up just clinging there
by what?
              By what by what ah yes by the skin
on the back of my hand I could not see focused as I was
using my nimble right hand my thrower to reach those few
inches and easy gently bring my awfully bent fingers
up like a soft hinge oh just to meet the palm and be even-
Stephen again yes this was important to make everything
exactly the way I recognized and stop the pearly
bubbles oozing from the slash it was hard to see so
calmly I called my wife to come unplug the screaming
saw could she hurry?
             The long freeze of time
odd how thinking time was a comfort just hold it time
out the time I needed to reach someone who could stop
no not stop simply sew up this what I still could not fix
a word or words an explanation to my bad my wrong my
stupid standing over the pine board whose odor roars
through my head a wooden hand no I want to go back and
practice practice practice cutting that two-by-four until
it comes out smooth and square to fit the fit the what was I
fixing what was I in such a hurry to make fit?

The dog
got there first all wound up squiggling his head jerking
his brown eyes so clearly worried is it his fault is it
the new house he needs before snow falls winds ice how odd
these thoughts firing yes yes it is your fault I yell
as my wife rushes in and no no I can see her mouth making
that shape no no I said it was me I did it calmly now
she pulled the cord the saw is quiet she is I believe
cooing her hands covered with flour what were you doing I
said making a pie she said can you walk?

Can I walk yes
but I want to dance slide over that golden sawdust to a
piano a subtle brush on the drums a smooth floor holding
this woman close intact whispering into her ear you're perfect
my angel tonight let me smell you your neck shoulders why
don't we glide down to the beach kick off our shoes the sky
is full of stars look at them flirting look I wanted to hold
her and hold her this isn't right is it this is crazy I am
seeing stars honey do you?

She is driving fast still cooing
no crooning to me passing cars a boy on a bike he wears a red
baseball cap turning hard a cardinal perched proudly see it
on the crown I always liked the Cardinals Dizzy Dean Stan
the Man Ozzie who did those beautiful backflips could scoop
up anything shortstops are wonderful to watch I once played
that position in Midget League was pretty good but your arm
they said is a pitcher's you've got control good control hum
babe hum I'm getting sleepy I say are we close?

Which is
only half-true the other half is throbbing how can I be
sleepy with these drums in my hand this woman asking me
sing sing come on I'll be down to get you come on get you
in a taxi baby come on please sing so I do I try god what a
great song isn't it romantic O say can you see by the dawn's
early mares eat oats and does eat oats and little lambs eat
see how good I can be?

                    All black now nothing no sun to play
under what do I love most nothing nobody I'm what exactly
a teacher you're a teacher a model yes I write words on
the board words help us clear up matters think feel under-
stand I like you I love you I love my hat my car hot dogs
with kraut I can't express exactly what I mean feel yes it's
hard it's beautiful too when just the right arrangement
gets close what's it like comfort a room hot soup your mother's
lips on your feverish forehead the glove beside you it's a
warmth isn't it warm?
                    The glove I wore summers was molded
part of me oiled and oiled a ball wrapped in it nights
by my bed hold me honey just hold on to me please I'm
slipping I remember counting backwards ten nine eight
seven yes I'd laugh at the girls hey Frankenstein's here
holding my glove up oh believe me I do not repeat do not wish
to drown soak myself I stink I stink I love my wife my dog
my words getting up each day so listen listen can you I'm
shouting hear me now?
                    You're dreaming baby wait here's
a towel wiping my chest my back I'm pouring night sweats
bring on this funny this very funny listen getting wet
gives me such a smooth easy hand I'm in the ocean creamy
you're so creamy you smell like nothing I've known a fish
no nothing like that still you squiggled snuggled flipped
and finally died I held you held you tight you tasted like
salt can't explain it let me sleep I'll try again I'll try
really come back honey come back okay?
                                        I know this I know
I put things where they belong dirty clothes straight
down the hamper empty bottles toothpaste capped newspapers
tied nothing wayward I sit at my desk a general ready picture
the occupant seizing a stray rubberband as if it might snap
Sloth loose in the neighborhood I'm so tidy so devoted to
order will I buy a supply of white gloves she says come on
come on Marine what a joker no matter what happens will you
I'm cold hold me?

Here's my plan it's very clear I toss softly
all my tools in the Goodwill box paint my desk green warm
hang African violets clematis grow grow I urge my tomatoes
Beefsteak Early Girls the window glass gleams the special
blue light hums vino sure why not a rich red I can make it
and maybe a child now look a boy a girl it doesn't matter
so many kids fall through the cracks no love we can save one
or two oh honey she says her eyes warm green I know this is
me now swimming up my lungs hurt can you see?
                                                    Look I
look at the stars my backyard blooms with them gushes
the cool green nights she puts her arms around me I didn't
hear you coming I say I'm lost in green green it's true
we can stop growing stop in the middle stop before the story's
had a chance to hint insinuate give a smile a sly wink sing out
keep us close like that breathing a little faster deeper
nothing so big we fall on our backs stunned do we need
to be stunned no she says just be be right here I say I know
that I promise I promise it's over she says all over can you
tell me can you see?
                            Look I know what I did how I am
it's true at the time but more true later always I need
to go back and use some good words at the rough spots like
sandpaper steel wool a file if I have to would you
give me your hand we're just walking along now starting
to court I love that verb to court one of us simply holds
out a hand the other is there if it's fine it is fine
look we're just walking along and it's starting yes I can
see.

A NEW SONG

In my daughter's room upstairs
we are sometimes stopped by a wasp
or two, or more, crawling across the warmed glass
of her sunny window—
sluggish things come from their winter cracks.

With my thumb
I break their necks
and brush them into an old shoe box
to toss outside.

She watches them flutter down to the orchard,
hugging her stuffed dog Blackie
and a book of poems she is too young to read—
though often she will sing from the book
to Blackie and me
a new song,

the one we have forgotten,
about the leafy wings blooming below
and floating up—up and up, always up—
to settle on our shoulders.

IN PIONEER PARK (*later*)

On the one swing in Pioneer Park
not broken, a boy and girl
taking turns pushing each other
are trying to reach the sky.
He wears her new baseball cap,
she his tattered wool sailor's,
their bare little legs at the highest arc
kicking clouds out of the way!
There are no clouds; the day is so clear
they can even see the Seven Devils' snowy peaks!
But clouds *must* be there, people
have to have clouds or it just isn't fair,
and a bear picking berries, showing
her children how, and a castle
no one is using right now.
They don't know why not. But they know
a great many things riding this swing—
they know almost *everything*—
like who used to jump up and run
from room to room, singing *Moon, moon,*
I do miss you so, boohoo, boohoo—
it was them! Margaret and James! Oh,
a long time ago, yes, she is quite sure,
they were very rich, they were orphans!
but not very tall. Maybe, maybe
one day they'll marry, who can tell? Who
can tell anything, isn't that scary?
Who? Who? Boohoo, boohoo. Oh,
please don't cry, not today, we're having fun
running away, higher, higher! Look,
look how far we've come!

WHERE THE DOG IS BURIED

Nights sometimes under the moon
I sit in my daughter's swing
and smoke; later I toss
the raw mound a little more
grass seed, a little more water.
If in the morning I find a mouse
beside my muddy boots on the deck,
I wing it into the valley, praising
the natural gifts of my cat, her cool
green eyes, and release.

These bright summer days when my daughter is here
I cast our line in the river and then place the rod
in her small hands. At night I read
from our book, feeling her warmth ease the ache
in my shoulder.
                        Over the graves of two quail
that broke their necks flying into my garden fence
I put up the sign she made: HOME CEMETERY. It's where
the dog I said ran away with a wolf
also lies buried. Waiting for sleep
I watch her reeling a rainbow in, see it flash, fly up, her joy
and relief as I kneel to cradle the fish in my shirt.

She was conceived in Czechoslovakia that famous year
of the Velvet Divorce, in the Slovak part, in the spring,
below the Tatra Mountains. Which the mountains around here
resemble so much, certain days, I feel both held still
and dizzy. I remember her mother and I often
ate trout, those slivers of sunlight and musky leaf
the tongue, when it's happy, catches up to.

The birds my daughter drew for her sign
are all in flight. Look at them,
she cries, pushing off between the two red fir perfectly
spaced for a good journey. When she goes out

far enough, flying over and over the cemetery,
the ropes sing. They both do—
and they are so in tune
you cannot tell one from the other.

CHRISTINA

The giant granite-gray shape
hovering over the church's portal
is Mary, her face a replica of so many
Holy Mothers I wonder why the artist
bothered, why he troubled himself
to fashion such a great mass
unless it was mainly for money.
I know that face, a sweetness
you barely glance at
to confirm that you stand once more
on familiar, reassuring, pious ground.
God save the saved among us—and give
the fallen air to breathe.

About to turn away, I hesitate:
the hands opening at my craned gaze
are monstrous, and how I nearly missed
the outrageous slap at scale
and comfort is suddenly painful.
These are not the pretty hands
you might implore to bring you
this or that and not in the far
future but now or soon or...
These are mean hands that dig
in the daily dirt, skin
roughened and aged and cracked
from the scratching through
to a better place,
the hands of a nobody, or of nobody much.

A refugee, an old soul
under a black shawl comes back,
Christina, no taller than her broom—
who rubs an onion on a boy's croupy throat,
who shows him keep-away-from-dogs,
who shows him over-such-fields
and how-to-fly.

Softly now she is cooing
a pullet into her skirts,
now raising her knuckled ruby
fingers up from a bucket
of hot bloody water, praising
all things good, toothless, blushing...

I do not know where she flew, finally.
I only know the chicken was stolen,
the halves of its boiled heart warm in their hands,
and how close they were on that stony ground
next to their little fire.

VISITATION NIGHT, DINNER FOR TWO

Our King Salmon Date, we call it,
no matter what's on our plates,
pasta, watermelon, the black olives
she mounts on her fingertips, to sing,
"I choose you...and you...and *you*..."
But this night it's true: a fresh
fillet I've baked with lemon and lots
of garlic—to keep witches and fibbers
with slitty eyes and nasty colds off our backs.
We like to flow smooth, to wiggle our tails
and leap up rivers until our hearts flip
among rainbows, till everything comes up true
as the fairy slippers we sometimes find
on our walks in the woods (when lucky's a thing
we can even behold). "As I was saying, my dear,
have you found any bones?" she inquires.
She is six. "Three, as a matter of fact."
"Oh, delightful, let's share—I found only one."
We finish with chocolate ice cream, double dips,
then I wash, she wipes, drying each fork and spoon
as if it's a prize for next time.
                              During our story upstairs
(which we reach thanks to our great silvery strides)
she holds her stuffed dog Blackie, my hand,
the plastic Baggie containing her two thin bones
and the one wish she's made twice—yes, of course
I know why: Once, that dunce, sometimes forgets it!
After the poor boy Lucky captures the Golden Feather
from the terrible griffin and can keep the king's
beautiful daughter, my little swimmer
is soon drifting off, happy that goodness wins out.
I give her two kisses, yes, just to make sure.

TRANSLATING MY POLISH MOTHER

I know her by now
like a book
or I'm a liar.
At eighty-three,
for example, she is not exactly
a pullet anymore,
and not exactly thrilled
to be outside
cleaning up
after a tree—
pushing all these damn leaves
and twigs into this old
packing crate—
and brushing away
a red curl.
Yes, it's real.
Maybe after a while
she'll open a cold Blatz
and watch the sky change color.
Her TV's on the blink.
Fine! What is it, anyway,
but a lot of *kupka*,
besides, everybody's either six
feet under
or too far away
or—What she'd like
to go with that beer
is a hunk of good dark
rye bread—or maybe
the thick one made with potatoes
nobody sees anymore—
and some pickled herring.
In the cream sauce
or plain, it's all
the same.
Now cut the bull,
get back, she'll quit
when her box is full.

AROUND THE CORRAL

"Sharks are very bitey,"
my daughter said,
climbing to the top
rail of our old corral,
"so we don't want any."
I stood beside her
leaning on my elbows,
gazing up the mountain
where a deer had been lying
crooked in a thicket
of spindly pine.
What was left of it—
the skull, hooves, a piece
of knuckly spine—
I buried. Somewhere
farther up, I imagined,
a lion stretched out silkily
and yawned, satisfied.
"What *do* we want?" I asked
and after a minute she said,
"A real good horse."
"A real good horse," I said,
"with a real good name,"
and she said, "Yes."
I said, "How about Razzle
Dazzle? How about Mister
Boom Boom? How about a name
that rolls across the land like
—like what?" "Like his
hair!" she said. "Like his
rocking chair!" "Like One
Happy Guy!" I said. "Like
Come On Home! Like Polish Bear!"
"So now we know," she said,
putting an arm around me.
"So now we do," I said.

JOSEPH SHOWS UP FOR THE CHRISTMAS STORY THREE DAYS AFTER HIS HERNIA REPAIR

In a white towel hiding his wild curls
and a sheet hanging from
shoulders to scuffed tennis sneakers,
Joseph waits among eight little girls
gathered below the chancel.
The closest two, not quite up to his chest,
wear wings he has to watch out for—
because they can't resist twisting
at the singing parts, or just suddenly
turning to show off their remarkable things.
He himself, stitched in the middle,
is being careful and thus stands still
like the good, patient witness
he is supposed to be anyway.
But you can see he feels deeply this role
of a man stunned, puzzled, and greatly honored
all more or less at once.
Even his mother—in the third pew
waiting with her camera, with her shiny
concerned-happy look that says
He seems so young to be a father!—
is at this moment no ordinary mother.
None of us is quite normal. Look at Mary
counting the fingers she can't
somehow get over—are they not wondrous?
Or is it time itself, the fabulous chain
from then to now to forever after
that makes her furrow that sweet brow?
The director plucks a reminder on her guitar
and the shepherds fix their gaze: a star
in the form of gold paper hangs down.
There is a miracle here somewhere,
or ought to be—and we are right.
"Behold!" Joseph calls out,
and hesitates, searching for his lines.

We wait. The place is so quiet
we could all be dead. *But please
do not worry about these closed eyes,*
his calm expression says, *I'm thinking.*
And who wouldn't be, under the circumstances?
Then he starts—and confidently, gloriously,
goes on without a hitch to the end.
It's this we remember afterwards
in our communal praise,
not what he said.

ENTER THE NORTH DAKOTA LIBRARIAN

whose eyes are a fair, spiky green
I only see on my hands
and knees at spring's initial offerings, how
can she help me? I say I seek the bloom
clarity achieves fending off confusion's weedy
waylays upon rich indirection, I hope
I won't be much trouble. Her lips forming
perhaps amusement, she tells me the tongue
of a woodpecker circles its brain
before coming out, and invites me to pursue
further, quietly. Gladly falling
to a whisper, noting a slight
shift in her hips, I wonder might her line be
French, it's the short boyish hair, the *poof*
in certain gestures of the hand. No, no,
whispering back, she's deep south and far north
to the bone, a hot and cool pearly mix,
which may help explain her passion
for the wolf, the solitude
of snow surrounding her every stride, and after
an evening's skiing crawling into the tent
she carries along no matter what
the temperature is, because she is also crazy
about the high view, about
Venus, Jupiter, Saturn, Betelgeuse, Aldebaran
and the Pleiades, whew, how faithful they are, over
and under, like wolves, you see, and sometimes
she can't bear to say *adieu*, raising one
not unfriendly auburn eyebrow. Mercy, where
are we? I venture. The Flickertail State, come
winter's dead center 70,000 square miles of often
chipped-tooth nights that call for more basil, more
sweet paprika in the marinara, pretty much where
we're headed, she says, the heart, that is,
of frost, upheaval. Adding she is a former
farmgirl who can take it, whose legs
were made firm running over the fields,

both away from and toward. Nearly breathless
I am still back at that saucy splice, the steamy
aromas I hunger for her rustic *cum*
bookish fingers to release rubbing fine
sundry herbals pleasuring our mixed portions,
both principal and adjacent. What do I know,
she inquires, about golden eagles? Absolutely
a minimum, I manage. The male,
she says, will pick up a stone—A small stone? I say—
Yes, she says, small, and will fly with it
maybe two hundred feet straight up
and then drop it—Drop it? I say—and she
says, Yes, and then will dive
down and catch it before it lands. I am
made weak in the thighs thinking how
hers made firm by rural-rearing were even
firmer now from striding under the stars, under
such a bright snatch. And now
clearly caught, she says, the female
eagle takes up the game but may
drop something entirely different: a clod
of dirt, a stick, even a dead squirrel
for we are, are we not, in the Flickertail
State—soaring, dropping, diving, catching,
they go, on and on—And then? and then?
I say. Then? she says, then? Why
they must meet, of course, and conclude,
she whispers.

for L.C.

WEAK STRONG

When the common flicker stitches
my chimney on a run of licks
every morning waking me *whap whap whap*
like a drummer so deep into the gig
he can't ever stop then stops and cool
aims his whammer straight up
listening a moment almost frozen
before turning his head this way and that
appearing nonchalant and then without
notice out flies a vocal
of just one note sounding more
human than birdlike over and over
plaintive pleading like *you-you-you*
I know it's only that feathered-up feeling
some of us will walk the floor
and bang our heads on anything
when it happens because
weak strong gripping a wormy tree
or a tin pipe it winds us round & round
and will not keep still until
we can bring the flicker of uncommon beauty
whose ear feathers are so fine she can hear
a heart being broadcast exactly like this
closer.

for Paula

A LITTLE PORTRAIT

Watching my gray
barn cat Yah teh circle
round and round
on her sunny bench
until she gets things
exactly right
is part of it—
and her unruffled
green-eyed glance
at the deer browsing
closer and closer
is another—
but the way you curl
a small lock
of hair
behind that ear
nearest the light,
watching me
watch you
let the lock
slowly slip
free,
completes it.

THE SUMMER AFTERNOON

The summer afternoon I sat on a roof, my mouth
full of nails, thinking about women as deeply
beyond me, one suddenly emerged from the door below
tendriled with vines and swayed across perfect buttons
of white clover like nothing I had seen before, not
like this, the honey-scent of pressed flowers released
and rising from her bare feet up past calves, passing
it on, refining it, to her thighs and hips until it joined
the nail juices sweetening my mouth in a swirl
my entire body was so richly marbled with I couldn't move
or swallow or let out breath or she would stop. I
didn't want her to ever stop, ever still
the skirt that seemed alive as heat trembling
on a road up ahead in fiery August, cold air crossing
over as I lay on my back on the ice holding Miller's Pond
together, dreaming between cracks shifting the surface
just slightly, cool soothing air made warm again
by the sun speckling in that auburn hair, hands moving
as if swimming, caressing, bathing the several layers
of prickly wrap somehow keeping the blood inside this fool-
ish exploding softly hard bag my body had become. I
finally managed, willed, a glance away to gather
breath, if breath is the word, so I could come
back to her stronger. She was walking out to fetch
her mail from a box under an arch ecstatic with purples
and pinks I later learned were clematis, a name whose three
parts I could bring to my tongue and slowly separate
to find the heart-shaped bud issuing velvet petals
in clusters that only wanted to twine and climb
over and over, I was fifteen or five or fifty, what
did it matter, she was simply the intricate total
of all those curves and lines I would never be able
to follow in the right order because they ran on
like a sentence out of its mind, kept moving around,
keep moving around, like water, wind, the same
wind I hear now and cannot stop, as I cannot stop her
from gliding through those curlicued vines again

after all these years, while the hushed sighs rush
among millions maybe trillions of needles in the red fir
crowns circling my house and the woman below me holds
my head between her long limbs whispering those nearly
lost notes, those sounds better than music, abandoned
to the genius of a song that started out whole
but is too overwhelmingly pure to stay that way.

G ary Gildner is the author of twenty books, including poetry, fiction, and memoir. His previous poetry collection, *The Bunker in the Parsley Fields*, won the Iowa Poetry Prize. His other awards include the William Carlos Williams and the Theodore Roethke, Pushcart prizes, and the National Magazine Award for Fiction. He has held fellowships from the NEA, Breadloaf, MacDowell, Yaddo, and Senior Fulbright lectureships to Poland and Czechoslovakia. He lives in Idaho's Clearwater Mountains.